18633

DEMCO

Ancient Greece

Don Nardo

KidHaven Press

KidHaven Press, an imprint of Gale Group, Inc.
10911 Technology Place, San Diego, CA 92127

18633

Library of Congress Cataloging-in-Publication Data

Nardo, Don, 1947–
  Ancient Greece / by Don Nardo.
    p. cm. — (History of the world)
Includes bibliographical references and index.
Summary: Discusses life in ancient Greece, including citizenship in
the city-state, family life, physical training and athletic competitions,
and religious beliefs and worship.
  ISBN 0-7377-0579-5 (alk. paper)
  1. Greece—Civilization—To 146 B.C.—Juvenile literature.
[1. Greece—Civilization—To 146 B.C. 2. Greece—Social life and
customs.] I. Title.
  DF77 .N372 2002
  938—dc21

2001004869

Copyright 2002 by KidHaven Press, an imprint of Gale Group, Inc.
10911 Technology Place, San Diego, California 92127

Printed in the U.S.A.

Contents

Chapter One

The Age of Heroes

Today Greece is a small country of modest means. But in ancient times it was the home of one of the most splendid civilizations in history. The ancient Greeks were very creative. They built magnificent temples, whose ruins are still visible across Greece. They also crafted beautiful statues of people and animals. In addition they also invented or perfected many of the ideas and institutions familiar today. One of these is **democracy,** the system of government in which people vote for their leaders. Theaters, plays, actors, and sports competitions like the Olympics are other Greek inventions. In addition, they developed the fields of science and **philosophy** (the attempt to understand the meaning of life).

Most of these achievements occurred in the fifth and fourth centuries B.C., about 2,300 to 2,500 years ago. Modern historians refer to that period as the Classical Age. And they call Greece's inhabitants in those days the Classical Greeks.

4

Ancient Greece

Athens, the leading Classical Greek city, located on a large peninsula in eastern Greece, was the first to experiment with democracy. The Athenians erected the famous Parthenon and other temples on their central hill, the Acropolis. Later ages came to see these monuments as the outstanding examples of the greatness of Classical Greece. Plutarch, a Greek writer who lived about four hundred years later, wrote that Athens's monuments "created amazement among the rest of humanity." They were the proof, he said, "that the tales of the ancient power and glory of Greece are no mere fables." [1]

The Mythical Age of Heroes

Yet despite the Classical Greeks' admirable works, they were not the first people to create a high civilization in Greece. And they were well aware of that fact. The ruins of huge, very ancient fortresses dotted their landscape. Moreover, their myths were filled with great heroes of the dim past. These larger-than-life figures had supposedly performed wondrous deeds and actually spoken with the gods. That is why the Classical Greeks called that long-ago legendary time the Age of Heroes.

One of the most famous heroes of that fabulous age was Theseus, a prince and later a king of Athens. Even way back then, the story goes, Athens was a leading city of mainland Greece. One of Theseus's myths tells about a sad and dangerous time for Athens. Each year, the king of Knossos, on the large Greek island of Crete, demonstrated his power over the mainlanders. He forced the Athenians to send him seven boys and seven girls. Then he fed the unfortunate youths to the Minotaur, a fearsome beast that was half-man and half-bull.

Determined to stop this outrage, Theseus traveled to

An ancient painted cup shows Theseus fighting the Minotaur.

Knossos. There, he bravely fought and killed the Minotaur and freed the hostages. His deed ended Cretan threats to Athens and allowed the city to go on to future greatness.

Greece's Bronze Age

It is natural to wonder whether these legends about Theseus might be true. Modern scholars are not sure if he was a real person. But they say it is possible that one of the kings of early Athens was named Theseus, and that over time he became a legendary character.

As for the story itself, the monstrous Minotaur is obviously not real. But some other parts of the tale may be based on true events. Today scholars know quite a bit more about very early Greek times than the Classical Greeks did. The so-called Age of Heroes

Minoan youths leap over the back of a huge bull in this painting from the palace of Knossos.

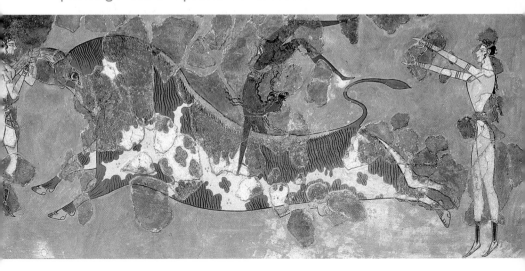

occurred about a thousand years before the Classical Age, in what historians now call the Bronze Age. **Bronze** is an **alloy,** or mixture, of the metals copper and tin. The era is so named because people used tools and weapons made of bronze.

Late in the Bronze Age, the region of Greece consisted of two general spheres. The first was Crete and other nearby Greek islands. The other was the Greek mainland. The islands were the home of a people modern scholars call the Minoans (named after one of their legendary kings, Minos). They built huge, splendid palaces, some of which were five stories high. Also, they had a large fleet of ships. For a long time they used these vessels to control the seas in the area. Perhaps they imposed their will on the mainland Greeks, as in the myth of Theseus. And the mainlanders responded by launching a military expedition against Crete.

Mainland Invaders and Farmers

Considerable evidence suggests that such an expedition did in fact occur. Historians call the early inhabitants of the Greek mainland the Mycenaeans. This name comes from their massive fortress-palace of Mycenae, situated on a rocky hilltop in southeastern Greece. The ruins of Mycenae are very impressive. They feature mighty walls made of stones so huge that years later the Classical Greeks thought giants must have erected them. Similar Mycenaean fortresses rose at Athens and other mainland sites. Sometime between

Part of the Minoan palace at Knossos still stands.

1500 and 1400 B.C., the Mycenaeans became strong enough to move against the Minoans. Evidence shows that mainland invaders took over Knossos and several other Minoan sites on the islands.

Whether they inhabited the mainland or islands, the Mycenaeans were mostly farmers. It appears that a local king owned much of the land surrounding his fortress-palace. A handful of wealthy nobles owned most of the rest. Only a few of the peasant farmers were landowners. The king and his advisers kept tight control of food production and levied taxes on each and every farmer. The farmers often paid these taxes with crops and livestock.

Writings on clay tablets found in the ruins at Knossos and other sites by **archaeologists** are proof

9

of how these ancient peoples lived. These tablets consist of long lists. On them are many individual names, probably those of peasants and other people who paid taxes. Measures of crops and livestock appear beside many of the names.

A Civilization Suddenly Falls

The Mycenaeans were sailors as well as farmers. After overcoming the Minoans, they became masters of the Aegean Sea, which borders eastern Greece. From time to time they raided other nearby coasts to acquire gold and other valuables. Such an attack may be the basis for the most famous of all the myths told later by the Classical Greeks—the Trojan War. Part of the tale became the subject of a long, colorful poem called the *Iliad*. Its author was Homer, a Greek who may have lived shortly before the start of the Classi-

A wall painting found on the island of Thera shows what may be Mycenaean ships and sailors.

The Trojan horse is said to have carried hidden Greek soldiers into Troy.

cal Age. In the story, a group of Greek kings attacked Troy, a prosperous city in Asia Minor (what is now Turkey). After many exploits by various heroes and gods, the Greeks pretend to give up. They give the enemy a gift of a huge wooden horse, which the Trojans drag into the city. That night some Greeks hiding inside the horse climb out and open the gates for the rest of the Greeks, who destroy the city.

Scholars are not yet certain that Homer's Trojan War was real. If it was, it was the last major expedition undertaken by the Mycenaeans. Beginning about 1200 B.C. or so, unknown invaders burned their fortresses. And for reasons that are still mysterious, their civilization rapidly fell apart. Greece entered a dark age of poverty and uncertainty. But fading memories of some of the heroes of the past remained. Their tales would help to shape a new and greater civilization that in the fullness of time would rise on Greek soil.

Chapter Two

The Long Road to Democracy

One of the ancient Greeks' most important achievements was the development of various political systems. The greatest of these was democracy. In a democracy, the people decide how the government should be run. Today more than eighty countries around the world are democracies. All of these nations owe a tremendous debt to the Greeks, especially to ancient Athens, where democracy was born.

The political experiments that led to the rise of democracy took several centuries. They began in the years following the collapse of the Mycenaean kingdoms at the end of the Bronze Age. Those kingdoms had been ruled by kings living in palaces. In the Dark Age, by contrast, life was centered around small villages. Each village had a chief called a *basileus*. Though he was the most powerful man in the community, he was something less than a king. He could not make all the decisions on his own. Instead, in really important matters he had to seek the approval of the village warriors. It was only a matter of time before more political power fell into the hands of ordinary people.

Political Experiments

Two important developments ensured that political experiments would continue in Greece. One was the increase of small farmers in the lands surrounding the villages. Unlike the peasant farmers of Mycenaean times, most of this new breed of farmers owned their own land. Also, they were not under the close control of a palace or other central authority. So they became very independent, both in their

A modern Greek farmer uses many of the tools and methods used by his ancient ancestors.

work and their thinking. They did not like being told what to do by the village chief or anyone else.

Even more important, these farmers were also the local warriors. If the community was threatened, they laid down their plows, donned their armor, and went out to fight. When the emergency was over, they returned to their farms. Sometimes these fighter-farmers got together to talk about community and political matters. This was called an **assembly.**

The Rise of City-States

The other important development was the transformation of simple villages into larger, more complex communities. Over time the new class of independent farmers grew increasingly successful. And trade with lands beyond Greece increased. These and other factors caused a rise in prosperity and an end to the Dark Age.

With the new prosperity, the villages naturally grew larger. Many became city-states. A **city-state** was a tiny country built around a central town. Usually (but not always), the town grew up around a steep hill. That hill was called an **acropolis,** meaning "the city's high place" in Greek. The people fortified it and retreated there in times of danger. The central town had a marketplace, where farmers from the surrounding countryside came to sell their crops. By about 700 B.C., two hundred years before the dawn of the Classical Age, hundreds of city-states had emerged across Greece.

Athens grew into a rich and important city.

Trying Various Political Systems

The Greeks called the city-state the **polis.** This is the term from which the word *politics* came. Indeed, on the long road to democracy, the city-states experimented a great deal with various political systems. Their efforts seemed to be living proof of a remark by a later Athenian thinker, Aristotle. "Man is by nature a political animal," [2] he said.

In most Greek states, the power first passed from the village chiefs to village councils. A typical council was composed of several local leaders. They met on a regular basis and decided on community policies together. They were usually the richest men in the community. Also, they saw themselves as the best

15

Athenian jurors discuss a legal case.

men in the community. So they became known as
aristocrats, a term that comes from the Greek word
aristos, meaning "best."

Some city-states were satisfied with their aristocratic councils. So they kept them for a long time.
But in other states, the small farmers and other common people grew discontented with the aristocrats.
In some cases, ambitious men saw in this discontent
a chance to gain great power. With the backing of the
common people, they replaced the aristocratic councils with one-man rule.

Such local "strongmen" became known as **tyrants.** Some ruled well and were very popular. Others abused their power, causing the term *tyrant* to take on the meaning it has today—an oppressive ruler. The Greek historian Herodotus described one famous tyrant—Polycrates, who seized power in the island polis of Samos:

> It was not long before the rapid increase of his power became the talk of the rest of Greece. All his [military] campaigns were victorious, his every venture a success. He had a fleet of a hundred and fifty warships and a force of a thousand bowmen. . . . He captured many of the islands and a number of towns on the mainland as well.[3]

Even successful tyrants like Polycrates did not last long, however. Such men needed the continued support of the people, especially the warriors, to stay in power. And increasingly, the people and their assemblies wanted to exercise that power themselves. The time was ripe for one city-state to take the fateful step and institute true democracy.

The World's First Democracy

Athens turned out to be the first Greek state to take that step, about 508 B.C. An Athenian aristocrat named Cleisthenes found himself in a power struggle with other local aristocrats. He asked for and got the

17

An Athenian citizen tries to sway a jury.

support of the common people against his opponents. Herodotus said that Cleisthenes "took the common people into his party. . . . And having gained their support, he found himself much more powerful than his rivals."[4]

In return for the people's help, Cleisthenes greatly increased the powers of the popular assembly. From then on, the citizens who met in the assembly voted to elect public officials. The assembly also had the authority to declare war, make peace, grant citizenship, and establish colonies. It even had the power to tell the generals what strategy to use in waging a war.

Another important aspect of Athens's new democracy was its fair justice system. A typical jury in a court case numbered four or five hundred members. Because of the large number, it was practically impossible for someone to use threats or bribes to influence the jury's decision. Any male citizen could bring a case to court. And a person was considered innocent until proven guilty of wrongdoing.

The people in many other Greek states were impressed by Athens's democracy. In the years that followed, a number of them installed their own democratic governments. Meanwhile, Athens grew

A modern painting recreates Athens's market area.

stronger and bolder. As Herodotus put it: "Athens had been great before. Now, having won her liberty, she grew greater still."[5] In addition to a strong democracy, Athens had an unusually large population and plentiful resources. It also possessed a large navy. Thanks to these and other factors, it would soon become the most active and accomplished city-state in Greece.

Chapter Three

Erecting Greek Temples

In the fifth century B.C., Greece witnessed an incredible outburst of cultural achievement. Never before or since has a single people produced so much in such a short time span. Magnificent religious temples, theaters, and other structures rose. And playwrights composed what are still viewed as some of the greatest plays ever written. Sculptors fashioned statues of rare beauty, while painting, pottery making, and other arts reached new heights.

A large portion of these accomplishments occurred in Athens. The most populous city in Greece, it was also the wealthiest. And its democracy allowed talented people almost total freedom to express themselves and create. For these reasons, the fifth century B.C. is often called the Golden Age of Athens.

Athena's Temples

Perhaps the largest and most enduring achievement of the Golden Age was the erection of religious

The Parthenon and other temples to Athena can be seen atop the rocky Acropolis.

temples in Athens and other Greek city-states. Large, impressive buildings, temples were the most common and distinctive communal structures in Greece. Some temples rose in the countryside, but most were located in the cities themselves, often in the marketplace or on the central acropolis or other hill. For example, the most famous group of temples in Greece stood atop the Acropolis at Athens. These structures were all built in honor of Athena. She was the goddess of wisdom and war, and also the city's **patron,** or special protector. By raising temples for her, the people hoped to maintain her favor. In the same way, the people of Corinth built temples for their own patron, Poseidon, god of the sea, and temples appeared in another important city-state, Argos, in honor of the goddess Hera, protector of women.

Each of these temples was shaped like a rectangle. The central section was a simple box with two main chambers. Surrounding the box was an enormous **colonnade,** or row of columns, each standing thirty feet high and weighing about a hundred tons. The

The small Temple of Athena Nike rests atop a platform on the western flank of the Acropolis.

roof was pitched (slanted) like that of a modern house. The roof's pitch created a large three-sided space on each of the building's ends. Inside these spaces, sculptors placed numerous statues. The statues were larger-than-life size and portrayed various gods in famous scenes from Greek mythology.

Workers Quarry and Transport the Stones

Erecting such large and beautiful buildings was a long and complex process. It typically took from ten to twenty years and employed hundreds, sometimes even thousands, of people. These included skilled craftsmen, as well as ordinary workers to assist them and do the heavy lifting. Plutarch listed such a group of workers assembled to erect a large temple, among them

> carpenters, coppersmiths, stone-masons, gold-smiths, ivory-workers, painters, and besides these the carriers and suppliers of materials, such as merchants, sailors, and pilots for the ships [that carried some of the materials to Athens], and wagon-makers and wagon-drivers [that carried other materials on land]. There were also rope-makers, leather-workers, and miners. Each individual craft . . . had its own army of unskilled laborers at its disposal.[6]

One of the first major steps undertaken by these workers was to cut the marble blocks and other stones needed to erect the temples. The stones came from quarries on the slopes of nearby mountains. Some of the quarry workers were slaves, but many were free men who received a small daily wage. To free the stones from the mountainside, the workers first carved grooves in the marble. They did this by striking metal chisels with wooden mallets. Next, they drove wooden wedges into the grooves. Then they poured water onto the wedges. The wood absorbed the water and the wedges expanded, forcing the stone to crack. Finally, the workers used crowbars to finish freeing the stones.

The Walls and Columns Slowly Rise

Huge wagons pulled by teams of oxen hauled the chunks of marble and other stones to a new temple's

A painting shows Greek workers laboring to erect a temple.

work site. Then the **masons,** experts at carving and building with stone, went to work. They trimmed and shaped the stones to fit in spaces that had already been measured. One common trimming tool they used was a short metal rod that was pointed at one end. Fittingly, it was called a **point.**

The masons cut the stones into different shapes. Those for the floor and walls were rectangular. By contrast, the stones for the columns were round. Each column was made up of a stack of such circular stones called **drums.** Whatever the shape of the stones, workers secured them to one another with small metal clamps.

As the walls and columns grew taller, the workers naturally had to lift the stones higher. They did this with simple but effective lifting devices. Each consisted of a series of sturdy wooden beams to which ropes and pulleys were attached. The workers also erected scaffolding around the sides of the unfinished structure. Scaffolding is a wooden framework supporting flat boards for workers to stand on.

Once the walls, columns, and roof were in place, the sculptors and painters climbed onto the scaffolding. Some sculptors put precarved statues in place. Others carved figures and designs directly onto the stones on the building's ends and sides. At the same time, the painters decorated both the structure and the statues with bright colors. Unfortunately, this paint is no longer visible. Many centuries of rain and wind have worn it away.

A Marvel to Behold

A finished Greek temple was a marvel to behold. Among the most beautiful and famous stone temples in Greece were those built for Zeus (leader of the gods) at Olympia, site of the Olympic Games; for Apollo (god of light and healing) at Delphi, in central Greece; and for Hera on the island of Samos. Unfortunately, the Temples of Zeus and Hera did not survive. And only the foundation and parts of a few columns remain of the Temple of Apollo.

However, a good deal more of the most spectacular and famous Greek temple of all—the Parthenon—has survived intact. The Parthenon, built atop Athens's Acropolis, was completed in the 430s B.C., at the height of the Golden Age. The city's leading political leader in the fifth century, a bold and talented man named Pericles, proposed and organized its construction. He hired the architect Ictinus to design the temple. Much of the stone used was a high-quality marble quarried on Mount Pentelicon, located about ten miles northeast of Athens. In all, some thirty thousand tons of marble went into the Parthenon's construction.

Little remains of the Temple of Apollo at Delphi.

27

Pericles' friend Phidias, the greatest sculptor of ancient times, designed the many statues that adorned the outside of the Parthenon. Phidias also supervised the erection of a huge statue of the city's patron, Athena, inside the temple. It was thirty-eight feet high and a stunning sight. The ancient Greek traveler Pausanias saw it and wrote:

The statue is made of ivory and gold. . . . [The goddess] wears a tunic that reaches the feet, and on her breastplate is carved the head of Medusa [a mythical monster]. In one hand

The Parthenon, symbol of the lost splendor of Ancient Greece.

Athena holds a figure of the goddess Victory about six feet high, and in the other she holds a spear.[7]

The finished Parthenon thrilled all who visited ancient Athens. And it has thrilled the world ever since. Over the centuries, the temple has suffered much from the effects of weather, vandalism, theft, and war. But large parts of its outer colonnade and a handful of its sculptures are still intact. Many of its other sculptures are in museums in Greece, England, and elsewhere. These magnificent remains, along with those of some other Greek temples, are the living truth of a prediction made by the great Pericles. "Future ages will wonder at us," he said, "as the present age wonders at us now."[8] Indeed, today people look back and marvel at Greece's Golden Age. And they are still awestruck at the sight of the majestic ruins on the Acropolis.

Chapter Four

The Decline of the Greeks

No sooner had Greece reached its height in the Classical Age when it began to decline. Eventually, the Greeks lost their power and influence and fell under the control of non-Greeks. This tragic series of events occurred mainly because the Greek cities never learned to get along. They frequently argued and fought among themselves. And their repeated wars caused a lot of bloodshed and destruction. Another result of these conflicts was that the city-states never managed to unite into a true nation. This left them weak and open to attack from an outside power.

The Defeat of Persia

The only time the Greek states achieved any kind of unity was at the beginning of the Classical Age. In 490 B.C., a few years after Athens introduced democracy, Persia attacked Greece. The huge Persian Empire was centered in the Near East, in what is now Iran. About ten thousand Athenian soldiers faced a much larger Persian army at Marathon, a few miles northeast of Athens. The Athenians won a resounding victory.

Ten years later the Persians returned with an even larger army. This time many Greek cities sent troops to defend Greece. The united Greek army defeated the invaders again and again. The Greeks' naval victory at Salamis, southwest of Athens, dealt a major blow. The Athenian playwright Aeschylus fought in the battle and later described it:

A Greek ship charged first and chopped off the whole stern [backside] of a Persian galley. Then charge followed charge on every side. . . . Then every Persian ship broke rank and rowed for its

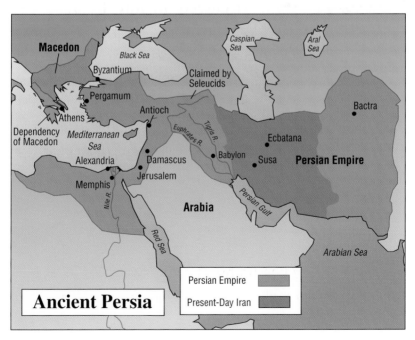

Ancient Persia

Persian Empire ▮
Present-Day Iran ▮

life. The Greeks seized broken oars and hacked and stabbed the Persians swimming in the sea.[9]

The Great War

Though the defeat of Persia was stunning, the Greek unity that had made it possible did not last. Two strong city-states had led the Greek resistance. One was Athens, which had Greece's biggest navy. The other was Sparta. Located in the Peloponnesus, the large peninsula making up southern Greece, Sparta had Greece's strongest land army. The two states distrusted each other intensely. They began to threaten each other, and from time to time they fought minor, largely indecisive battles.

Greek and Persian warships fight it out in the naval battle of Salamis.

Finally, the rivalry between Athens and Sparta led to all-out war in 431 B.C. Almost all the Greek states entered the fray. Some backed Athens, while the rest fought for Sparta. According to the Athenian historian Thucydides, who fought in the conflict: "The two sides were at the very height of their power and preparedness, and I saw too, that the rest of the Greek world was committed to one side or the other. . . . This was the greatest disturbance in the history of the Greeks." [10]

The terrible conflict became known as the Peloponnesian War (because Sparta and its major allies were in the Peloponnesus). Many Greeks called it the Great War. It lasted for twenty-seven grueling years and caused much death and devastation. Sparta and its allies eventually won. Athens's cultural Golden Age ended, and for a while the city lost its cherished democracy.

The Rise of Macedonia

In the years following the Great War, Athens and its allies recovered. But the Greeks had not learned that disunity and war were foolhardy. Soon the city-states were at one another's throats again. More costly battles and wars ensued.

Beginning in the 340s B.C., Macedonia saw its chance to take advantage of the bickering city-states. Macedonia was a kingdom located in northern Greece. Its king, Philip II, created a large and very strong army and defeated the strongest city-states.

A mosaic found at Pompeii in Italy shows Alexander the Great in the midst of battle.

Philip wanted to unite the Greeks at last. He planned to lead them in an invasion of Greece's old enemy, Persia. But one of his own subjects suddenly murdered him. So his young son, Alexander III, ended up launching the expedition. A skilled and shrewd general, Alexander conquered the immense Persian Empire in only a few years. A later Greek historian, Arrian, wrote: "No nation, no city, no individual was beyond Alexander's reach. Never in the world was there another like him." [11] Later generations agreed and came to call him Alexander the Great.

The Conquest of Greece

Unfortunately for Greece, Alexander died at the age of thirty-three in 323 B.C. In the usual Greek spirit of disunity, his officers immediately started fighting one another, and his huge new empire rapidly fell apart. A series of destructive wars followed and lasted for about forty years.

When these conflicts ended, Greece and the Near East looked very different. Three large Greek kingdoms had emerged. One, the Macedonian Kingdom, ruled most of mainland Greece. Another, the Seleucid Empire, covered a large portion of the old Persian realm. And the third, the Ptolemaic Empire, was made up mainly of Egypt.

The leaders of these kingdoms now made the same fatal mistake their ancestors had. They repeatedly

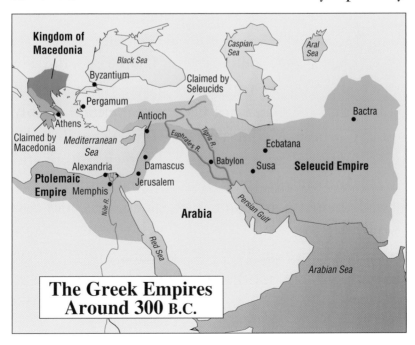

The Greek Empires Around 300 B.C.

Greek citizens bow to their Roman conquerors.

fought one another for control of the region. Once again, war and disunity made the Greeks weak and open to invasion. This time, the threat came from far to the west. The Romans, masters of the Italian peninsula, had recently conquered the lands of the eastern Mediterranean, and now they turned on the Greeks. A Greek named Agelaus made a desperate plea for unity. "It would be best," he said, "if the Greeks never went to war with one another." They should now "speak with one voice and join hands like men crossing a river." [12]

But this call fell on deaf ears. The Greeks did not unite, and Rome swiftly conquered them. It was Rome, therefore, and not Greece that ended up ruling the whole Mediterranean world. The Romans were impressed and fascinated by Greek culture and ideas. And luckily they absorbed these things and passed them on to later ages. But Greece did not know liberty or self-rule again for over two thousand years. It was not until the 1830s that a true nation of Greece emerged.

Notes

Chapter One: The Age of Heroes

1. Plutarch, *Life of Pericles*, in *Parallel Lives;* excerpted in *The Rise and Fall of Athens: Nine Greek Lives by Plutarch*. Translated by Ian Scott-Kilvert. New York: Penguin, 1960, p. 177.

Chapter Two: The Long Road to Democracy

2. Aristotle, *Politics*, in *Introduction to Aristotle*. Edited by Richard McKeon. New York: Modern American Library, 1947, p. 556.
3. Herodotus, *The Histories*. Translated by Aubrey de Sélincourt. New York: Penguin, 1972, p. 220.
4. Herodotus, *Histories*, pp. 364–65.
5. Herodotus, *Histories*, p. 364.

Chapter Three: Erecting Greek Temples

6. Plutarch, *Life of Pericles*, in *The Rise and Fall of Athens*, pp. 178–79.
7. Pausanias, *Guide to Greece*, in *The Art of Ancient Greece: Sources and Documents*. Edited and translated by J. J. Pollitt. New York: Cambridge University Press, 1990, p. 56.
8. Quoted in Thucydides, *The Peloponnesian War*. Translated by Rex Warner. New York: Penguin, 1972, p. 148.

Chapter Four: The Decline of the Greeks

9. Aeschylus, *The Persians*, in *Aeschylus: Prometheus Bound, the Suppliants, Seven Against Thebes, the*

Persians. Translated by Philip Vellacott. Baltimore: Penguin, 1961, p. 134.

10. Thucydides, *The Peloponnesian War,* p. 35.

11. Arrian, *Anabasis Alexandri,* published as *The Campaigns of Alexander.* Translated by Aubrey de Sélincourt. New York: Penguin, 1971, p. 398.

12. Quoted in Polybius, *Histories,* published as *Polybius: The Rise of the Roman Empire.* Translated by Ian Scott-Kilvert. New York: Penguin, 1979, pp. 299–300.

Glossary

acropolis: "The city's high place"; a central hill around which many Greek towns were built. The capitalized version—Acropolis—refers to the one in Athens.

alloy: a mixture of two or more metals

archaeologist: one who studies archaeology, the science of digging up and studying past civilizations

aristocrats: "best men"; people belonging to a community's wealthy, privileged class

aristos: "best"

assembly: a meeting in which local citizens discussed and debated issues and/or voted for leaders

basileus: a chief or "head man" of a village or town, mainly during Greece's Dark Age

bronze: an alloy composed of the metals copper and tin

city-state: a small nation built around a central town

colonnade: a row of columns

democracy: a form of government in which the people vote for their leaders

drum: one of several circular stones stacked to form a column

mason: an expert at carving and building with stone

patron: A god or goddess thought to provide special protection to a city

philosophy: the attempt to understand the meaning of life and the way the world works

point: a pointed metal tool used by masons to trim stones

polis: a city-state

tyrant: a leader who acquired power in an unlawful way, usually by seizing it with the help of soldiers and/or other local citizens

For Further Exploration

Isaac Asimov, *The Greeks: A Great Adventure.*
Boston: Houghton Mifflin, 1965. An excellent,
entertaining overview of Greek history and
culture.

David Bellingham, *An Introduction to Greek
Mythology.* Secaucus, NJ: Chartwell Books, 1989.
Explains the major Greek myths and legends and
their importance to the ancient Greeks. Contains
many beautiful photos and drawings.

Peter Connolly, *The Greek Armies.* Morristown, NJ:
Silver Burdette, 1979. A fine, detailed study of
Greek armor, weapons, and battle tactics, filled
with colorful, accurate illustrations. Highly
recommended.

Denise Dersin, *Greece: Temples, Tombs, and
Treasures.* Alexandria, VA: Time-Life Books,
1994. This handsome volume has an excellent,
up-to-date, and beautifully illustrated chapter on
Athens's Golden Age.

Homer, *Iliad.* Retold by Barbara Leonie Picard.
New York: Oxford University Press, 1960; and
Odyssey. Retold by Barbara Leonie Picard. New
York: Oxford University Press, 1952. Easy-to-
follow, quick-moving introductions to Homer's

classic works, which shaped Greece's mythology and national character.

Joanne Jessup, *The X-Ray Picture Book of Big Buildings of the Ancient World*. Danbury, CT: Franklin Watts, 1993; and Mike Corbishley, *The World of Architectural Wonders*. New York: Peter Bedrick Books, 1996. These colorfully illustrated volumes, aimed at young readers, each have a section on the Parthenon, the magnificent Temple of Athena erected atop Athens's Acropolis.

Charles Kingsley, *The Heroes*. Santa Rosa, CA: Classics Press, 1968. Presents superb retellings of the famous ancient Greek myths of Jason and the Golden Fleece, Perseus and Medusa, Theseus and the Minotaur, and the labors of Heracles (Hercules).

Don Nardo, *Greek and Roman Theater*. San Diego: Lucent Books, 1995; *The Age of Pericles*. San Diego: Lucent Books, 1996; *The Parthenon*. San Diego: Lucent Books, 1999; *Greek and Roman Sport*. San Diego: Lucent Books, 1999; *Life in Ancient Athens*. San Diego: Lucent Books, 2000; and *The Ancient Greeks*. San Diego: Lucent Books, 2001. These books, which are aimed at junior high and high school readers, provide a great deal of information about ancient Greek history and culture.

Susan Peach and Anne Millard, *The Greeks*. London: Usborne, 1990. A general overview of the history, culture, myths, and everyday life of ancient Greece, presented in a format suitable to young, basic readers.

Jonathon Rutland, *See Inside an Ancient Greek Town*. New York: Barnes and Noble, 1995. This colorful introduction to ancient Greek life is aimed at basic readers.

Index

Picture Credits

About the Author

A historian and award-winning writer, Don Nardo has written and edited numerous books about ancient Greece. Among these are *The Age of Pericles, Life in Ancient Athens, Greek and Roman Sport,* and Greenhaven Press's massive *Complete History of Ancient Greece.* He lives with his wife, Christine, in Massachusetts.